The Charismatic

LUTHER

Healings, Miracles and Spiritual Gifts
in the Life of the Great Reformer

Eddie L. Hyatt

HYATT PRESS * 2016

*Publish, and set up a standard; publish
and conceal not* (Jeremiah 50:2)

THE CHARISMATIC LUTHER
By Eddie L. Hyatt
© 2017 by Hyatt International Ministries, Incorporated
ALL RIGHTS RESERVED.

Published by Hyatt Press
A Subsidiary of Hyatt Int'l Ministries, Incorporated

Mailing Address:
P. O. Box 3877
Grapevine, TX 76099-3877

Internet Addresses
Email: dreddiehyatt@gmail.com
Web Site: www.eddiehyatt.com
Social Media: Eddie L. Hyatt

Unless otherwise indicated, all Scripture quotations
are taken from the New Kings James Version of the Bible. ©
1979, 1980, 1982 by Thomas Nelson, Inc. Publishers.
ISBN: 978-1-888435-57-3

Printed in the United States of America

About the Author

Dr. Eddie L. Hyatt is a seasoned minister of the Gospel with over 45 years of ministerial experience as a pastor, Bible teacher, and Professor of Theology. He holds the Doctor of Ministry from the School of Divinity at Regent University, and has a passion to see this generation impacted by genuine Spiritual awakening. He is the author of numerous books on revival and reformation, including *2000 Years of Charismatic Christianity*, which is used as a textbook in colleges and seminaries around the world. His books are available from Amazon and from his website. Eddie resides with his wife, Dr. Susan Hyatt, in Grapevine, TX where they are establishing the Int'l Christian Women's Hall of Fame and Ministry Center.

Contact Information. If you would like to correspond with Eddie for any reason, including invitations to speak, you may do so at any of the following:

Email: dreddiehyatt@gmail.com
Website: www.eddiehyatt.com
Social Media: Eddie L. Hyatt
Mailing Address: P. O. Box 3877, Grapevine TX 76099

Table of Contents

Preface

October 31, 2017 marked the 500-year anniversary of Martin Luther nailing his 95 Theses to the Wittenberg Church door and igniting the Protestant Reformation. Although no one at the time could have imagined the impact of this act, it turned out to be an epochal event that changed world history.

Many people have been impacted by Luther's life, even in modern times. In 1934, for example, Michael King, Sr., a black pastor from Atlanta, Georgia, travelled with a group of Baptist pastors to the Holy Land and then attended a week-long Baptist World Alliance conference in Berlin. While in Germany, King and others visited many of the religious, historical sites related to Luther and his work.

King was so inspired by the life of Luther that upon returning home he changed his name to Martin Luther King, Sr. and changed the name of his five-year-old son to Martin Luther King, Jr. The rest is history.

I too have been inspired by Luther's life and message, and that is the reason for writing this book. It is written for a general audience that would like to know more about Luther's life and significance. Having been a participant in the modern Pentecostal and charismatic revivals, I have purposely given special attention to Luther's experiences with miracles and Spiritual gifts. I have also included a chapter on his confrontations with false miracles and pseudo prophets.

5

At a critical time in Israel's history, God instructed the nation, through the prophet Isaiah, to take a look back from whence He had brought them. He said,

> *Look to the rock from which you were hewn and to the hole of the pit from which you were dug. Look to Abraham your father and to Sarah who bore you* (Isaiah 51:1-2a).

As you, through this book, look back to the rock from which the Protestant Reformation was hewn, and the pit from which it was dug, it is my prayer that you will be inspired to trust God for new expressions of revival and reformation in the days ahead.

Chapter I

The Early Years

I pray you, leave my name alone and do not call
yourselves Lutherans, but Christians. Who is Luther? My
doctrine is not mine. I have not been crucified for anyone.
Martin Luther

Martin Luther (1483-1546) was born on November 10, 1483 in Eisleben, Germany into a hard-working family from the lower classes of German society. Luther remembered his mother carrying wood from the forest on her back and he said that both parents "worked their flesh off their bones" to bring up seven children.

Luther was never ashamed of his rustic upbringing, but rather valued and esteemed it. He once said to his friend, Melanchthon, "I am a peasant's son; my father, grandfather and all my ancestors were genuine peasants."[1]

When he was six months old, Luther's parents, Hans and Margaret, moved ten miles from Eisleben to Mansfield, which is situated about 125 miles southwest of Berlin. Hans became employed in the copper mines and some think he may have managed or even shared in ownership of the mines, for he was able to acquire property and achieve a measure of prosperity.

The World of Luther

The world into which Luther was born was not

characterized by kindness and tolerance, but by harshness and intolerance. To believe the wrong thing was a civil crime, known as "heresy" and punishable by death. One-hundred years before Luther, the Czech priest/pastor, John Huss, preached that the Bible, not the pope, is the ultimate authority for the Christian. He was tried, found guilty of heresy and publicly burned at the stake.

Indeed, since the time of Constantine, who merged the church with the state, the church had more and more relied on civil power rather than gospel persuasion to maintain and expand its cause. Considering the Roman organizational genius, it is no surprise that the church in Rome took on a highly complex and organized structure that in many ways reflected the structure of the Empire.[2]

Following in the steps of the Roman emperor, the bishops of Rome expanded their power over other churches and eventually became the dominant force in Europe through the papal office. Popes declared that in the same way the moon derives its light from the sun, kings and emperors derive their right to rule from the pope.

Secular rulers often disagreed claiming that the pope and bishops derived their authority from the civil ruler. This "investiture" conflict came to a head in the 11th century when King Henry IV of Germany began installing bishops in his area.

Pope Gregory VII responded by excommunicating Henry, releasing all his subjects from any obligation to him and ordering them not to serve him as king. This had a powerful effect on all of Germany and with his kingdom slipping from him, Henry, with his wife and young son, crossed the Alps in the dead of winter to beg forgiveness from the pope who was residing at Canossa.

Gregory refused to see Henry at first, requiring him to wait for three days in the bitter cold at the gate of the palace, barefoot and dressed in simple garb. When Henry was finally allowed into the pope's presence, he knelt before him and begged forgiveness and to be received back into the church.

There also developed through the Roman Church a sacramental system by which God's gifts of salvation and grace were imparted through outward rites such as baptism, the Eucharist, confirmation, etc. These rites, however, were only valid if administered by a duly ordained priest of the Roman Church.

By these and other religious mechanisms, the masses were held in bondage and fear to a complex religious system. And with the Bible outlawed in the vernacular languages of the people, they were held captive by the Roman Church with seemingly no way of escape.

A Man for the Times

By the time of Luther, however, there was widespread unrest and dissatisfaction with the abusive authority of the popes and the Roman Church. In addition, a pietist movement in the thirteenth and fourteenth centuries had nurtured a desire for more heart and less form in worship. But who would dare challenge this powerful religious system that had subdued both kings and emperors?

The answer was Martin Luther, and he came on the scene like a John the Baptist, denouncing the sins of the Roman Church hierarchy and calling the people back to the Scriptures and to the Christ of Scripture. Although rough, bold and bombastic when confronting the ills of the church, it was exactly what was needed. A "nice" person would never have prevailed against the entrenched systems of power that prevailed in the 16th century.

Early Life & Education

Luther's parents were devout Roman Catholics who taught their children to pray to God, Mary and the saints, and to revere the church and the priests. They went regularly to mass and there was an air of superstition in their faith, for Luther remembered frightful stories they told about the devil and witches--stories that stayed with him the rest of his life.

Hans and Margaret were also strict disciplinarians and his mother once chastised him until the blood came for stealing a single nut. His father once beat him until he fled away. Luther said he recognized their good intentions, and in spite of the severe discipline, he always cherished family affections.

His education began in the local elementary schools where, in addition to the rudiments of reading and writing, he learned the Apostles' Creed, the Ten Commandments, the Lord's Prayer and several Latin and German hymns.

At age eighteen he entered the University of Erfurt where he studied what was known as the seven liberal arts. These included grammar, rhetoric, logic, arithmetic, geometry, music and astronomy. Luther completed these studies in one year and received his Bachelor of Arts in 1502. He continued his studies and completed his Master's degree in 1505.

According to his father's wishes, Luther now enrolled in law school. His father's plans for him to become a lawyer were, however, suddenly disrupted by a dramatic occurrence that happened during a return journey from his home to the university.

During the approximate fifty-mile journey on foot, Luther was caught in an intense thunderstorm. In a moment of panic, he cried out to St. Anne, promising that if his life was spared he would become a monk. True to his vow, and the distress of his father, he entered the Augustinian monastery in Erfurt.

His First Exposure to the Bible

It is likely that Luther enrolled in law school because of the desire of his father, not his own, and that the "thunderstorm experience" provided the excuse, or reason, to go in a more "spiritual" direction.

That his heart was inclined to knowing God rather than studying law was obvious when he saw a complete Bible for the first time in the university. He opened it with a sense of awe and later told how he was surprised, "and rejoiced to find that it contained so much more than was ever read or explained in the churches."[3]

Bibles were rare because the printing press had been invented only about forty years before Luther's birth. Bibles were also rare because laws were in place throughout Europe forbidding the masses to own a Bible in their mother tongue.

In the 12th century, for example, Pope Innocent III declared that in the same way God ordered that the beast that touched the holy mount was to be stoned to death (Exodus 19:12-13), "so simple and uneducated men were not to touch the Bible or venture to teach its doctrines."[4]

In 1486, Archbishop Berthholdt of Germany echoed Innocent's ban of Scripture, declaring,

> The Scriptures are not to be given to simple and unlearned men and, above all, are not to be put into the hands of women."[5]

Luther obviously longed to study the Bible. He also longed to find peace with God for his troubled soul and joining the monastery seemed the only path available for such a pursuit.

Life as a Monk

Luther entered the monastery believing that he would never leave it. He gave himself completely to that life, and later said, "I never thought of leaving the convent: I was entirely dead to the world, until God thought that the time had come."[6]

With a small cell containing a hard, simple bed, a chair and a desk, Luther gave himself completely to the austere lifestyle of a monk. He arose at 2 a.m. every morning to engage in the saying of the Lord's Prayer and repeating the Ave Maria during the seven appointed hours of prayer.

In his zeal to be a saint and make his salvation sure, Luther went beyond the required discipline of the convent. He engaged in extended times of prayer, meditation, fasting, vigils, night watches and other religious exercises. He was held up as a model of sanctity by his fellow monks and later wrote, "If ever a monk got to heaven by monkery, I would have gotten there."[7]

But in spite of his best efforts, he was still tormented by a sense of corruption in his heart and the fact that he had no peace with God. It was not a particular sin that he could identify, but sin as a corruption of nature and a sense of alienation from God that distressed his mind and brought him to the brink of despair.

While in the monastery, Luther was sent back to the university to get his Doctorate of Theology degree. This meant that he could learn Greek and Hebrew and study the Bible in the original languages. He was thrilled for this was what he had longed to do since the day he had picked up the Bible for the first time in the university.

This was also significant preparation for his life work in which he would call the church back to the Scriptures. And even now, as he studied the Bible for himself, he could see the discrepancy between what Jesus and the Biblical writers taught and what he had been taught and what the church of his day taught.

Luther was awarded the Doctor of Theology degree in 1507, and ordained to the priesthood that same year. He remained a part of the monastery but took on the extra duties of a priest in preaching and hearing confessions.

Luther Moves to Wittenberg

In 1508, Luther was assigned to teach theology at the University of Wittenberg, a small, insignificant town of only three-thousand inhabitants. Its claim to fame lies exclusively in the fact that it is the town that gave birth to the Reformation, and it reminds us of Paul's words in I Corinthians 2:27, *God has chosen the foolish things of the world to put to shame the wise, and God has chosen the weak things of the world to put to shame the things which are mighty.*

Luther continued to live the monastic lifestyle in Wittenberg and most of the professors were members of his monastic order. Luther both preached in the town church and taught courses on Bible and theology in the university.

Although the student body was at first small, students would eventually come from far distances to study at Wittenberg because of the influence of the Reformation and Luther's fame throughout Europe. Luther's friend and colleague at the university, Philip Melanchthon, said he heard as many as eleven languages spoken around his table.

Among the courses he taught, Luther was assigned to teach the New Testament books of Romans and Galatians, letters of Paul that emphasize faith for salvation as opposed to the works of the law. These letters captivated his thinking and highlighted the contrast of his own external efforts to gain salvation with what the Scriptures taught about salvation through faith in Christ apart from the works of the law.

He was particularly drawn to Romans 1:16-17 where Paul writes,

For I am not ashamed of the gospel of Christ for it is the power of God to salvation for everyone who believes, for the Jew first and also to the Greek. For in it the righteousness of God is revealed from faith to faith; as it is written, "the just shall live by faith."

The words of verse 17, *the just shall live by faith*, particularly captured his attention. He would often quote those words, especially after the Holy Spirit thundered them in his heart during a visit to Rome in 1510.

His Visit to Rome

In the autumn of 1510, Luther's superior, Johann Staupitz, sent him to Rome to deal with a matter related to the monasteries. The whole journey must have taken several months, and Luther and his two companions were hosted in monasteries as they made their way to Rome.

At this time, Luther is still a devout Catholic with a romantic view of Rome as the great, holy city of saints and martyrs. As he, therefore, came into view of the city for the first time, he raised his hands and exclaimed, "Hail to thee, holy Rome!"

His perception of Rome as a holy city was, however, shattered as he beheld the corruption, vice and immorality that had taken over the city. Schaff says he was "shocked by the unbelief, levity and immorality of the clergy."[8] Luther later said that he received the impression that, "Rome, once the holiest city was now the worst."[9]

This experience exacerbated the war that had already begun to rage in his soul between his Roman Catholic upbringing

15

and training, and what he was personally learning from the Scriptures. Tradition was still strong enough that he decided to make the most of this trip to Rome and acquire some special indulgence or blessing while there.

Luther, therefore, went to a shrine called the Scala Sanata, a set of marble stairs famous for the supposed indulgences that could be obtained by climbing its twenty-eight steps on one's knees. He hoped to obtain some tangible blessing by this penitential act.

The word of God, however, was also at work in Luther's heart and mind. As he climbed the stairs on his knees, he seemed to hear with every step the words of Romans 1:17, *The just shall live by faith*. He rose to his feet with a new sense of the reality of faith alone being necessary for acceptance with God.

Luther returned to Germany obviously affected by what he had seen and experienced. He later would say that he would not have missed seeing Rome for anything for it removed any apprehension he may have later felt for attacking the papacy and the Roman Church.[10]

The Times are About to Change

At Wittenberg, Luther continued his pastoral and teaching duties, still a committed Roman Catholic with no thought of every leaving the Roman Church. At the same time, however, he was growing in his own personal faith and seeing the need for serious change and reform in the church of which he was a part.

Later in life, he revealed that there came a moment when he

suddenly saw that righteousness, or acceptance with God, was not something one can earn, but a gift given to the sinner who puts his/her faith completely in Christ. It was like the morning sun suddenly dawned in his soul, and he wrote,

> All at once I felt that I had been born again and entered into paradise itself through open gates. Immediately I saw the whole of Scripture in a different light.

This was an important and timely milestone in his spiritual journey for he would need this revelation in the days ahead as he challenged long-held beliefs. This understanding of the righteousness of God through faith was the basis of his decision in 1517 to publicly challenge the selling of indulgences, which offered forgiveness of sins and freedom from hell and purgatory, all for a price.

Chapter 2

Conflict with Rome

When the pope acts contrary to the Scriptures, it is our duty to stand by the Scriptures, to reprove him and to restrain him, according to the word of Christ.

Martin Luther

With Luther's rough and bold temperament, and his acquisition of knowledge concerning the gospel, an explosive conflict with Rome was almost certain. Certain conditions in Europe and Germany in 1516-17 provided the setting for this conflict to come out into the open in full force and fury.

Tetzel and the Sale of Indulgences

Johann Tetzel, a representative of the pope, was travelling throughout Europe selling indulgences for the building of St. Peter's basilica in Rome. An indulgence offered forgiveness of sins, all for a price. It also offered release from purgatory and hell for both the purchaser and their departed loved ones.

The more serious the sin, the higher the cost of the indulgence. However, the seriousness of the various sins was obviously based on church dogma, not Scripture. For example, murder and incest were about one-half the price of assaulting a priest and less than one-third the price of imitating the pope's handwriting.[11]

Tetzel was considered a theologian, but he was also a cunning promoter and marketer of his goods. He would enter a town with great pomp and pageantry. Priests, monks, magistrates, and crowds of people would meet him at the edge of the city and march with him to the parish church where he would set up shop.

Underneath a large cross and a banner bearing the papal arms was placed a large chest for receiving money from the sales. Being the consummate salesman, Tetzel had a saying, "When the coin in the coffer clings, a soul from purgatory springs."

With the masses cut off from personal exposure to the Scriptures, they were left at the mercy of such mercenary, religious thievery. And with the church teaching that only the pope and his bishops possessed the divine gift from God to understand and teach the Bible, they were further alienated from any basis by which to challenge this corrupt system.

Luther Challenges with 95 Theses

By this time, however, Luther had arrived at a place in his spiritual journey that he knew that such merchandising of the gospel was abusive and unbiblical, and he could no longer be silent. He, therefore, wrote out 95 short statements, or theses, by which he challenged, on Biblical and reasonable grounds, the selling of indulgences.

On October 31, 1517, Luther nailed his 95 Theses to the Wittenberg church door. This was parallel to a modern posting on a social network and he called for a public discussion or debate of the issue. People not only came to the church and read his theses, but they were printed and spread throughout Germany.

Opposition Arises All the Way from Rome

This act set off a firestorm of debate both in public and in writing between Luther and Catholic authorities. On August 7, 1518, Luther was ordered to appear in Rome within 60 days to recant his heresies. On August 23, the pope demanded the German prince, Frederick the Wise, to hand over this "child of the devil" to Roman authorities.

Frederick, however, was sympathetic to Luther. He, therefore, negotiated for a meeting in Augsburg, Germany between Luther and the papal representative, Cardinal Cajetan.

Luther and Cajetan had three meetings on October 12, 13 and 14. Cajetan demanded that Luther retract his "errors" and confess absolute submission to the pope. Luther resolutely refused to do so saying that he could do nothing against his conscience, and quoting Acts 5:29, he declared that one must obey God rather than man.

The discussions ended with Cajetan threatening excommunication. He also urged Staupitz, Luther's superior in the monastery, to do his best to convert Luther and stated that he was unwilling to have any further discussion with this "deep eyed German beast filled with strange speculations."[12]

Between June 27-July 15, 1519 Luther participated in another debate with Johann Eck who had attacked Luther's teachings and accused him of reviving the "Bohemian heresy" of John Huss. The debate was held in the large hall of the Castle of Pleissenburg at Leipzig, under the auspices of Duke George of Saxony. It gained widespread attention and thrust Luther even further into the limelight.

The debate centered on the authority of the pope and the infallibility of the Roman Church. Eck quoted primarily from church fathers and church tradition, while Luther quoted primarily from Scripture. A person who presided at the debate, wrote of Luther, "His learning and his knowledge of the Scriptures are so extraordinary that he has nearly everything at his fingers' ends."[13]

Luther argued that the claim of primacy by the Roman bishop (pope) as the successor Peter, was contrary to the Scriptures and contrary to the early church. In the debate he also insisted that church councils were not infallible, especially the Council of Constance that had condemned John Hus.

This was a turning point for this was the first time he had openly challenged the authority of the pope and church councils. This put him on an obvious collision course with Rome and he knew that only God could save him.

The Prophecy of John Huss

After the debate at Leipzig, Luther received a letter from the followers of John Huss in Bohemia. Huss (1369-1415) was a Czech priest who served as dean and rector of Charles University in Prague. In 1415 the Council of Constance tried him and found him guilty of heresy, and he was burned at the stake the same day.

These followers of Huss also sent a small book summarizing Huss's views. When Luther read it, he was astounded for Huss had preached that Christ, not the pope, was head of the church. He also emphasized the authority of Scripture. In amazement, Luther declared, "We are all Hussites without knowing it."[14]

It is likely that it was from these same individuals that Luther learned the story of Huss's prophecy at the time of his execution. Although some scholars discard this story, there is sufficient evidence to accept it as fact if you are not predisposed against such predictive prophecy.

Huss is said to have spoken this prophecy as he was being led to the place of execution. In Bohemian, the word "Huss" sounds like "goose," and with a play on words, Huss declared to those who were watching, "They will roast a goose now but after a hundred years they will hear a swan sing, and him they will endure."

Luther obviously drew encouragement from this prophecy, for he quoted it early-on in one of his writings, and then said, "And that is the way it will be, if God wills."[15]

He Articulates His Message

With supporters and representatives of the pope now attacking and threatening excommunication, Luther began the serious work of putting his thoughts in writing. In 1520 he wrote two books, *To the Christian Nobility of the German Nation* and *The Babylonian Captivity of the Church*, in which he laid out the need for reform and relentlessly attacked the papal office and the Roman Church system.

Knowing he needed God's help in these endeavors, Luther bathed his study and writing in prayer. His prayer life was confirmed by one of his close associates, Veit Dietrich, who stayed with Luther in Coburg during the Diet of Augsburg in 1530. According to Dietrich, Luther began his day with three hours of fervent prayer. He wrote,

> No day passes that he does not give three hours to prayer. Once I happened to hear him praying. How great a spirit, how great a faith, was in his very words! With such reverence did he ask, as if he felt he was speaking with a Father and a Friend. My mind burned within me with a singular emotion when he spoke in so friendly a manner, so weightily, so reverently, to God.[16]

In these books of 1520, Luther began by expressing his felt need for God's protection and help. For example, in the introductory section of, *To the Christian Nobility of the Christian Nation*, he wrote,

> The first and most important thing to do in this matter is to prepare ourselves in all seriousness. We must not start something by trusting in great power and human reason, even if all the power of the world were ours. For God cannot and will not suffer that a good work begin by relying on one's own power and reason. He dashes such works to the ground as it says in Psalm 33:16, *No king is saved by his great might and no lord is saved by the greatness of his strength.* I fear that this is why the good emperors Frederick I and Frederick II and many other German emperors were in former times shamefully oppressed and trodden underfoot by the popes, although all the world feared the emperors. It may be that they relied on their own might more than on

God, and therefore had to fall.[17]

In these books Luther proceeded to lay out the need for reform, and in doing so, he fearlessly attacked the Roman Church system. In *The Babylonian Captivity of the Church*, for example, he wrote,

> Therefore, no one is obliged to obey the ordinances of the pope, or required to listen to him, except when he teaches the gospel and Christ. And the pope should teach nothing but faith without any restrictions. But since Christ says, *He who hears you* (plural) *hears Me* (Luke 10:16), why does not the pope also hear others? Why does not an unbelieving pope now and then hear a believing servant of his who has the word of faith? Blindness, sheer blindness reigns among the pontiffs.[18]

When Frederick the Wise suggested that he moderate his tone, Luther replied,

> The more those Romish grandees rage, and mediate the use of force, the less do I fear them, and shall feel all the more free to fight against the serpents of Rome. I am prepared for all, and await the judgement of God.[19]

Luther's proactive message consisted of three major components: (1) *sola fide* (faith alone); that we are saved by faith alone apart from church appointed indulgences, sacraments, penances and the like; (2) *sola Scriptura* (Scripture alone); that the ultimate authority for the Christian is the Bible, not church tradition, councils or the pope; and (3) *the priesthood of all believers* by which he

24

insisted that everyone is a priest and may go to God apart from the priestly, mediatorial system of the Roman Church.

With this kind of bold resistance to ecclesiastical authority and tradition, it was only a matter of time before the hammer would fall and he would be excommunicated.

Luther's Excommunication

On June 15, 1520, Pope Leo X issued a papal bull (official decree) giving Luther sixty days to recant or be declared a heretic. Luther received the document on October 10, meaning he had had until December 10 to respond.

Luther was not fazed. He was convinced he was on the side of truth and in a letter to Frederick the Wise, stated, "Your Grace knows, if not, I make known to you, that I have the gospel, not from men, but from heaven through our Lord Jesus Christ."[20]

Therefore, on the morning of December 10, Luther's students built a large bonfire. Luther then publicly burned the papal bull, the Roman canon law and other books supporting the pope. It was an open and defiant act against the pope and the Roman Church.

Leo responded by announcing Luther's formal excommunication as of January 3, 1521. He referred to Luther as "a wild boar" that had invaded the Lord's vineyard. Excommunication was also threatened against anyone who would harbor Luther or his friends.

All princes and magistrates were ordered to seize Luther and his followers and turn them over to the Roman authorities. Christians were ordered not to read, print or publish any of Luther's books, but instead to burn them, and such occurred in many cities

Because Frederick the Wise with his army was protecting Luther, the pope was reluctant to try and arrest him. He, therefore, called on Charles I, the Roman emperor, to give legal force to Luther's excommunication.

"Here I Stand"
Luther's Bold Stand at Worms

After negotiations with Frederick the Wise and other civil and religious rulers, Charles I agreed that Luther would appear before a civil/religious court in the German city of Worms. Frederick also negotiated a "safe conduct" from the Emperor meaning that he agreed not to arrest Luther in his travels to and from the Diet.

It was at the Diet of Worms that Luther drew a line in the sand and made his stand for truth and righteousness, which would change world history.

It was an impressive tribunal before which Luther was ordered to defend his teaching. The emperor in all his royal dress and entourage was there along with bishops, cardinals, personal delegates of the pope, dukes, princes and counts, all in their splendid garb and titles. Schaff called it "a fair representation of the highest powers in Church and State—a numerous array of dignitaries of every rank."

In contrast, Luther was dressed simply in his monk's cowl as he faced this imposing court. It was David versus Goliath multiplied a hundred times over.

A table had been placed in the room with Luther's books on

it. He was first asked if these were his books. He looked them over and replied in the affirmative. He was then ordered to recant.

It seems that Luther may have been momentarily rattled by the intimidating show of pomp and power he faced. In a voice that could barely be heard, he asked for more time to consider the demand of recantation. Schaff, however, thinks his request was not out of fear but out of seriousness, knowing the gravity of the situation.

The emperor gave Luther one day to consider the order, and he returned to his lodging where he spent much of the night in prayer. During the night, there came into his heart a fearlessness and boldness such as the apostles must have experienced when they stood before the Jewish authorities and boldly defended their faith in Jesus (Acts 5:29-32). Later in life Luther wrote about that moment, saying, "I was fearless. I was afraid of nothing. God can make one so desperately bold."[21]

Luther returned the next day and was again ordered to recant. He stated that he was willing to recant but only if he could be shown by Scripture and reasonable arguments that he was wrong. Knowing his life was on the line, Luther did not flinch, but quietly and confidently stated,

> I consider myself convicted by the testimony of Holy Scripture, which is my basis. My conscience is captive to the Word of God. Thus, I cannot and will not recant anything, because acting against one's conscience is neither safe nor sound. Here I stand! I can do no other! God help me! Amen!

The proceedings were over and Luther returned to his lodgings, where he threw up his arms and joyfully shouted, "I am through, I am through!" Knowing that many "heretics" before him had been beheaded, he exclaimed, "If I had a thousand heads, I would rather have them all cut off one by one than make one recantation."

After further deliberations, the court affirmed the pope's excommunication of Luther as a heretic. Anyone knowing his whereabouts was to inform the nearest authorities so that he could be arrested and brought to justice.

Luther, by this time, had already departed. On his way to Wittenberg, friends with their faces masked, kidnapped him and took him to a castle known as Warburg in the German forest. Their actions were ordered and arranged by Frederick the Wise who did not trust Charles's guarantee of a safe conduct.

Frederick were aware that the emperor Sigismund had given a similar safe conduct guarantee to Huss but broke his promise and had Huss burned at the stake the same day. The Council of Constance justified Sigismund, saying that one was not required to keep his word to heretics.

Luther was in hiding for approximately one year during which time he translated the New Testament from Greek into German. He eventually returned to Wittenberg and resumed his pastoral duties, and his writing and teaching. By this time, the Reformation had gained such widespread support that neither the pope nor emperor would dare attempt an arrest of Luther.

In later life, when asked how he, a simple monk and teacher, had been able to have such an impact when opposed by both the pope and the emperor, Luther replied,

> I simply taught, preached, wrote God's Word; otherwise I did nothing. The Word so weakened the papacy that never a prince or emperor did such damage to it. I did nothing. The Word did it all.[22]

Chapter 3

Miracles &
Spiritual Gifts

*Often has it happened, and still does, that devils
have been driven out in the name of Christ; also by
calling on His name and prayer, the sick have been healed.*

Martin Luther

One of Luther's first biographers, Johann Mathesius, mentions various prophecies spoken by him which were fulfilled and then remarks, "With many sure prophecies he confirmed his doctrine."[23] Many of Luther's early followers, in fact, believed him to be a prophet. Even Melanchthon at one point referred to Luther as Elijah, saying, "Thus the Holy Spirit prophesied of this third Elijah, Dr. Martin Luther."[24]

Luther is sometimes thought to have been against the miraculous ministry of the Holy Spirit. This misconception has come about for at least two reasons. First, he wrote against the superstition and greed that had become associated with the miracles of the medieval Roman Catholic Church. Secondly, he opposed certain Anabaptists who claimed the direct leading of the Spirit for their bizarre teaching and actions.

Contrary to this, however, Luther left clear evidence of his own belief in the personal and direct ministry of the Spirit. In his book, *Luther and the Mystics*, Professor Bengt

Hoffman, of Lutheran Theological Seminary in Gettysburg, Pennsylvania, tells of a conversation in which Johann Cochelus asked Luther if he had received special revelations. Luther was silent for a moment, and then replied, "'*Est mihi revelatum*,' yes, he had had revelations." According to Bengt, it seems that one of these was similar to Paul's experience of being caught up to the third heaven (2 Cor. 12).[25]

Luther's Source of Authority

Luther also claimed the direct activity of the Holy Spirit as a source for his own authority and teaching. In his book, *The Babylon Captivity of the Church,* he assured his readers that the truth he was presenting, "I have learned under the Spirit's guidance."[26] In addition, when he was challenged concerning the source of his authority by church and civil officials at Worms, "he relied on the revelation of God to him—through the Word, but via the Spirit in a personal manner."[27]

This writer vividly recalls his first reading of Luther's own writings and the impact it produced. As I read *The Babylonian Captivity of the Church,* I was amazed at the clear, concise and bold nature of his message and said to myself, "Luther is speaking with apostolic authority."

Luther, of course, would never call himself an "apostle" or "prophet" for his boldness came, not from his person, but from the message he had rediscovered. He considered the Christ-centered message of justification by faith and the priesthood of all believers to be "apostolic" and he was willing to defend it with his life.

Luther and Divine Healing

Luther regularly prayed for the sick, and even composed a divine healing service for Lutheran congregations. He is quoted as saying, "Often has it happened, and still does, that devils have been driven out in the name of Christ; also by calling on His name and prayer, the sick have been healed."[28]

When his wife, Katy, became seriously ill after a miscarriage, Luther and others prayed fervently for her. He later said that it was the power of prayer that kept her alive and allowed her to recover relatively quickly.[29]

On another occasion, Luther's close friend and colleague, Philip Melanchthon, became extremely ill and was at death's door. Luther is said to have fervently prayed, using all the relevant promises he could repeat from Scripture. Then, taking Melanchthon by the hand, he said, "Be of good courage, Philip, you shall not die."

Melanchthon immediately revived and soon regained his health. He later said, "I should have been a dead man had I not been recalled from death itself by the coming of Luther."

On another occasion, Luther received word that his friend and colleague, Frederick Myconius, lay dying in the last stages of tuberculosis. When Luther prayed for his friend, he obviously experienced a manifestation of the gift of faith spoken of in I Corinthians 12:9-10. This is obvious from the letter he wrote to Myconius in which he said,

> I command thee in the Name of God to live because I still have need of thee in the work of

reforming the Church. The Lord will never let me hear that thou art dead but permit thee to survive me. For this I am praying, this is my will, and may my will be done because I seek only to glorify the Name of God.[30]

Myconius said that when he read the letter it seemed as though he heard Christ say, "Lazarus, come forth!" Luther's prayer and declaration were fulfilled. Myconius was healed and outlived Luther by two months.

In his book, *The Babylonian Captivity of the Church*, Luther challenges the sacramental system of the medieval Roman Church. In addressing the sacrament of Divine Unction, which is based on James 5:14-15, Luther laments that this promise of healing has been turned into a rite for the dying. He challenges his readers to embrace the original purpose of this passage and then says,

> Who prays over the sick one in such faith as not to doubt that he will recover? Such a prayer of faith James here describes, of which he said at the beginning of his epistle: *But let him ask in faith, with no doubting* (James 1:6). And Christ says of it: *Whatever you ask in prayer, believe that you receive it, and you will* (Mark 11:24). There is no doubt at all that, even if today such prayer were made over a sick man, that is, made in full faith by older, graver, and saintly men, as many as we wished would be healed.[31]

Miracles Not Confined to Luther

The emphasis on the miraculous ministry of the Holy Spirit

was by no means limited to Luther. Johannes Brenz, another Lutheran reformer, was warned by an "inner voice" of the approach of the Spanish army at Stuttgart. The inner voice instructed him to go to the upper city, find an open door, enter it and hide under the roof. He obeyed, found the door and hid as the voice had instructed. His hiding place was visited by a hen that daily laid two eggs for him until the danger was past.[10]

Luther's Role in Cessationism

In spite of his obvious belief in the immediate presence and power of the Holy Spirit, Luther must share some of the blame for the widespread belief in a theory of the cessation of miracles that emerged in the Reformation.

When challenged by Roman Catholic authorities to perform miracles on demand to prove his authority, Luther took refuge in the authority of Scripture and his own conscience. Miracles, he argued, were particularly suited to the apostolic age and were no longer necessary to vindicate the authority of the one who stands on the side of Scripture.[32]

Interestingly, Luther presented the same Catholic demand to certain Anabaptists who, in his opinion, maintained an undue reliance on visions and miracles, and neglected the study of the word of God.

Sadly, his remarks were taken out of context by later theologians and codified into a legal system resulting in Lutheran and Reformed churches harboring a distinct bias against the possibility of present-day miracles.

The Holy Spirit Among Modern Lutherans

In spite of these unfortunate trends, Luther's original example was not lost and the twentieth century witnessed a new receptivity of the Holy Spirit among modern Lutherans. In 1987, for example, the International Lutheran Renewal Center coordinated an international, thirty-two-member Lutheran Theological Consultation, which produced *Welcome, Holy Spirit: A Study of Charismatic Renewal in the Church.*

This study shows a marked receptivity to the charismatic dimension of the Spirit. Although it questioned certain traditional Pentecostal doctrines, it acknowledged that Pentecostals "have accurately perceived the Spirit's strategy" in that He is "calling believers to receive a personal outpouring of the Holy Spirit," and calling them to be "filled with the Holy Spirit in a way and to a degree that they have not done before."[33]

Luther would, no doubt, agree. The fourth stanza of his great hymn "A Mighty Fortress Is Our God" contains the phrase, "The Spirit and gifts are ours." Souer's work in German, *A History of the Christian Church,* on page 406 of volume 3, describes Luther as "a prophet, evangelist, speaker in tongues and interpreter, in one person, endowed with all the gifts of the Holy Spirit."[34]

Chapter 4

False Miracles
& Pseudo Prophets

The miracles that happen in these places prove nothing, for the evil
spirit can also work miracles, as Christ has told us in Matt. 24:24.
Martin Luther

The Reformation opened the door to all sorts of wild
theories about the church, the end of the world, the
kingdom of God and how it would be established. Some
said the kingdom of God would be established by God's
people taking up the sword, slaying the wicked and
establishing righteousness by force. Others said God's
kingdom would be established by a "second
commissioning" of apostles and prophets who would go
forth with such power, signs and wonders that no one
would be able to resist them.

In addition to these extremes in the Reformation, there were
also the purported miracles within Catholic mysticism and
monasticism that Luther felt obligated to confront. Whether
Catholic or Protestant, all of these groups placed great stress
on supernatural dreams and visions, at the expense of
Scripture, as the basis for their bizarre doctrines and
behavior.

The False Miracles Within Catholic Mysticism

The medieval mystics, who often functioned within the monastery or convent, testified of many sensational miracles and revelations. However, they tended to neglect the Scriptures, which left them open to deception. Referring to this problem in Catholic mysticism, the modern Catholic theologian, Hans Kung, writes,

> These new revelations not only overshadowed the Bible and the gospel, but also Him whom the gospel proclaims and to whom the Bible bears witness. It is striking how rarely Christ appeared in all these "revelations," "apparitions," and "wonders." Catholics who followed in the wake of every new "revelation" . . . and yet had never once in their whole lives read the Scriptures from cover to cover.[35]

In his book, *To the Christian Nobility of the German Nation,* Luther severely rebuked Catholic Church leaders for promoting such extra-Biblical miracles, and profiting by them. These false miracles included claims that certain hosts (*i.e.,* communion wafers) bled and that a statue of the Virgin Mary had been miraculously created.

Great crowds flocked to the places where these alleged miracles were supposed to have occurred and much money was collected in offerings, in fees for masses, and from the sale of amulets and indulgences. Luther was incensed and thundered his rebuke:

> Oh, what a terrible and heavy reckoning those bishops will have to give who permit this devilish deceit and profit by it. They should be the first to prevent it and

yet they regard it all as a godly and holy thing. If they had read the Scripture as well as the damnable canon law, they would know how to deal with this matter! The miracles that happen in these places prove nothing, for the evil spirit can also work miracles, as Christ has told us in Matt. 24:24.[36]

A False Spirituality in the Reformation

Luther also found it necessary to confront extreme elements in the Reformation itself, whose proponents gave more value to inner thoughts and impressions than to the written word. This, of course has been a problem in every revival movement in history. John Wesley, Jonathan Edwards, George Whitefield and all evangelical revivalists have had to deal with this issue of how to strike a healthy balance between Word and Spirit.

As the Reformation gained momentum, Luther was confronted with various people and situations representing differing sorts of deception and extremes. The Reformation was dramatic, exciting and powerful, but it was also messy, painful and at times chaotic.

The Prophets of Zwickau

While Luther was hiding in the Castle of Wartburg, after his condemnation at the Diet of Worms, three men from Zwickau, known as the Zwickau Prophets, visited Wittenberg. Led by a weaver named Nicholas Storch, they claimed divine visions, dreams and visits from the angel Gabriel.

They were part of the congregation in Zwickau where Thomas Muntzer was priest, a position he occupied based on a recommendation from Luther. Muntzer, however, fell into deception and began proclaiming himself a new prophet who would usher in a new dispensation by the sword. He would later meet a terrible end wherein he and fifty-three of his followers would be tortured and then beheaded.

In the meantime, Storch and his two friends wowed the people with their revelations and began taking the reform movement in Wittenberg in a radical direction that was not compatible with Luther's desire or with Scripture. Luther was for gradual change as a result of the people's hearts being changed by the preaching of the word.

These new prophets, however, demanded instant and radical changes in the church services and the long-held traditions and practices of the people. They began smashing statues, images and paintings. Their basis of authority was not Scripture, but the visions and angelic visitations, which they claimed.

Although many, including some of Luther's colleagues, were won over by the sensational claims of these men, their presence and message caused unrest in the city, prompting Melanchthon to send a message to Luther about what was happening.

When Luther read the message, he put his life at risk, left the Castle at Wartburg, and returned to Wittenberg. Frederick the Wise, concerned for his safety, wrote to him expressing concern and demanding an explanation for leaving his place of security. Luther's reply reveals the heart of a pastor and shows how he was truly moved by a deep concern for the church and his own people in Wittenberg. He wrote,

> During my absence Satan has entered my sheepfold, and committed ravages which I cannot repair by writing, but only by my personal presence and living word. My conscience would not allow me to delay longer; I was bound to disregard, not only your Highness's disfavor, but the whole world's wrath. It is my flock, the flock entrusted to me by God; they are my children in Christ. I could not hesitate a moment. I am bound to suffer death for them, and will cheerfully with God's grace lay down my life for them, as Christ commands (John 10:12).

Upon his return, Luther preached eight sermons on eight consecutive days, challenging with Scripture the visions and dreams of the prophets from Zwickau. The noted historian, Philip Schaff, wrote, "In plain, clear, strong, scriptural language, he refuted the errors without naming the errorists."[37] Luther then wrote a small book entitled *Against the Heavenly Prophets* in which he showed that the inner, subjective work of the Spirit must always be subject to the objective word of God and common sense.

It was in this battle with the "Prophets of Zwickau" that Luther coined the word *schwarmer* as a derogatory designation for these individuals whom he considered to be irrational dreamers led astray by the feelings and imaginations of their own heart.

My Personal Encounter with a *Schwarmer*

This writer is reminded of how, during the midst of a series of meetings, he received a phone call from one of the participants. The voice on the other end of the line said, "I was lying by the pool meditating and God spoke to me and said, 'Call Eddie Hyatt and tell him to start a church and call it 'The Gateway to Heaven.'"

I did not need a special revelation from heaven to know that the message was not from God. I also knew he was not a false prophet, just a mistaken one who had not learned to distinguish the voice of the Spirit of God from his own thoughts, feelings and over-active imagination. He was a *schwarmer*, but an honest one who was willing to receive correction.

The *Schwarmer* Leave Wittenberg

The *schwarmer* in Wittenberg, however, were unwilling to receive correction. Nonetheless, through Luther's preaching, it soon became obvious to the people that the "prophets" were in error. Realizing they had lost their influence, the three men departed Wittenberg. One of Luther's colleagues wrote to the Elector of that region,

> Oh, what joy has Dr. Martin's return spread among us. His words, through divine mercy, are bringing back every day misguided people into the way of truth. It is as clear as the sun, that the Spirit of God is in him, and that he returned to Wittenberg by His special providence.

Although Luther was not prefacing what he said with a "thus

41

saith the Lord," his message was obviously more prophetic than the dreams and visions of the *schwarmer*. He based his message on God's word rather than inner, subjective thoughts, feelings and impressions, which, he insisted, must always be subject to the outer, objective word of God.

The Revelation of Christ in Scripture

Luther's approach to testing the spirits by Scripture came into play one day when, during prayer, he suddenly saw a shining vision on the wall of Jesus, with the wounds of His passion, looking down upon him. He thought at first that it was a heavenly vision, but changed his mind when he noted that the person in the vision was not compatible with the Christ he knew from Scripture. He said,

> Therefore, I spoke to the vision thus: "Begone you, confounded devil. I know no other Christ than He who was crucified, and who in His Word is presented unto me." Whereupon the image vanished, clearly demonstrating from whom it came.[38]

Luther's experience reminds us of the Emmaus Road experience of Jesus with two of his disciples in a post-resurrection appearance (Luke 24:13-35). During this approximate two-hour walk from Jerusalem to Emmaus, Jesus spent the entire time taking them from Genesis to Malachi and showing them Himself throughout the Old Testament. Luke says, *And beginning with Moses and all the Prophets, He expounded to them in all the Scriptures the things concerning Himself* (Luke 24:27).

It was obviously very important that these early disciples know the Christ of Scripture so as not to be led away by a mystical or spiritual Jesus that is divorced from Scripture. Luther, a diligent student of Scripture, learned the importance of this in his own experience.

He Lived by God's Word

Luther tested everything by the Scriptures, and he emphasized the centrality of Christ. Anything that would diminish Christ was to be avoided. In discussing the canon of Scripture, he once said,

> All the genuine sacred books agree in this, that all of them preach and inculcate Christ. And that is the true test by which to judge all books. For all the Scriptures show us Christ, Romans 3; and St. Paul will know nothing but Christ, I Corinthians 2:2. Whatever does not teach Christ is not apostolic.

For Luther, the Bible was both his guide and source of strength. The noted historian, Philip Schaff, said of Luther, "He lived and moved in the heart of the Scriptures; and this was the secret of his strength."[39]

Chapter 5

Marriage, Family & Final Days

There is no more lovely, friendly and charming relationship, communion or company than a good marriage.

Martin Luther

Even after renouncing his vow of celibacy as a monk and priest, Luther still had no intention of marrying. His mind was taken up with continual debates, writing and his duties as a priest and professor. He also had discounted marriage because he thought at any time his fortunes could change and he could be put to death as a heretic.

It was, therefore, a surprise to everyone, including, himself, when marriage seemed to be thrust upon him. He wrote to a friend, saying, "Suddenly, and while I was occupied with far other thoughts, the Lord has plunged me into marriage."

A Wife Finds Luther

It all began with a letter from a young nun in a convent telling him about how she had read his writings and believed what he preached. She also said that she and other nuns in the convent wanted to leave the convent but since they were bound by law to their vow of celibacy, she asked for his advice on how to proceed.

Luther arranged for a merchant, who delivered fish to the convent, to smuggle them out—twelve in all—in the fish barrels in his covered wagon. They were brought to Wittenberg where, over time, Luther helped each one find a husband or a vocation, except one, Katharina von Bora, the one who had written the letter.

Of a feisty and assertive character, Katharina stated that there were only two men she was interested in marrying, Nicholas von Almsdorf or Martin Luther. When Almsdorf turned down the offer, Luther decided to take it. He made the decision he said, "To please my father, rile the pope, cause the angels to laugh, and the devils to weep."

After a very short engagement, Luther and "Katy," as he called her, were married on June 13, 1525. He was forty-one and she was twenty-six.

Luther was obviously very happy in his marriage and in later life, wrote,

> I would not want to exchange my Kate for France nor for Venice to boot; to begin with (1) because God has given her to me and me to her; (2) because I often find out that there are more shortcomings in other women than in my Kate; and although she, of course, has some too, these are nonetheless offset by far greater virtues; (3) because she keeps faith and honor in our marriage relation.

Katy's Role in the Lutheran Household

Katy has been described as "healthy, strong, frank, intelligent and high-minded." She managed the Lutheran household, which included their own six children, four cousins, an aunt, twenty-five or more students who boarded with them, servants and a constant stream of visitors. One of Luther's colleagues said he had seen as many as one hundred people at the Lutheran home for a meal.

Katy managed everything, including the finances. She raised livestock and chickens. She had an extensive garden, or farm, all used for feeding her extensive household. She was a good manager and able to procure enough money to purchase her brother's part in the family estate known as Zulsdorf, which she then owned and managed.

Love and Respect

Luther related to Katy both respectfully and affectionately. In his letters he referred to her as "my dearest" and himself as "your loved one." Because of her leading role in the household, he often referred to her as "herr" Katy, "herr" being a German word of respect meaning "lord" or "master." He also referred to her as "Moses" and at times signed his letters (I am sure all in fun), "your willing servant."

He also used the word "Lady" in referring to her, which was a civil term of respect for a woman of nobility, influence and authority. One can see his playful humor in some of the titles he gave her. For example, because of her business and farming skills, he sometimes called her "Lady of the Pig Market." Because she spent so much time at her family estate he called her "Lady of Zulsdorf" and because she was continually giving him home remedies for his many illnesses he called her "Lady Doctor."

They obviously had their differences, but Luther never tried to pull rank or set up a marriage hierarchy. He once said,

> Oh, how smoothly things move on when man and wife sit lovingly at table! Though they have their little bickerings now and then, they must not mind that. Put up with it!"

Luther realized how blessed he was to have someone who was gifted in areas he was not. He noted that before his marriage, his bed sheets were not changed for a whole year and he admitted to being a "negligent, forgetful and ignorant housekeeper." He was thankful for Katy and her gifts that left him free to focus on teaching, traveling and writing.

Luther's Children

Luther took great joy in his marriage and his children, with whom he would often play. When he was away for extended periods of time, they would write him letters, and he would return home with little gifts for them.

Katy bore three sons and three daughters. Two daughters died at a young age, one at seven months and the other, Magdalene, at age thirteen.

Magdalene's death was particularly difficult for Luther. Magdalene, whom the family called Lena, was a lovely child with whom he often "made merry." During her sickness Luther talked to her openly about the possibility of death and asked if she was willing to leave her earthly father and go to her heavenly father. She replied, "Yes, dear father, just as God wills."

On the night of her death a friend observed Luther kneeling by her bed, weeping and asking God to spare her life. She died in his arms. Expressing his conviction that she was with the Lord and would rise again, Luther stated with tears, "I am rejoicing in the spirit but I am very sad according to the flesh."

At the funeral, as they laid her body in the coffin, Luther stated that it was well with his beloved daughter and that she would rise again. He then was overcome with sobbing.

A Step Forward for Marriage

Luther's attitude toward marriage was a large step forward from that of the medieval period, for which he and Katy deserve much credit. His rejection of celibacy as a requirement for ordination undermined the medieval idea that women are sinister and unclean and detrimental to a life committed to God.

This sort of thinking about womanhood and marriage was popularized by the famous African church father, Augustine, who in the fifth century taught that the woman does not bear the image of God apart from the man. The man bears the image of God in himself alone, Augustine said, but the woman only when she is related to the man.

In explaining the meaning of the word "helper" in Genesis 2:18, Augustine surmised that the woman could not be a helper in physical and manual labor since a man would be a better help. And when it comes to fellowship and dialogue, Augustine insisted that a man's companionship is preferable to that of a woman. He concluded that the only way the woman is a "helper" to man is in bearing children and thereby helping him perpetuate the human race through the sex act.

In her book, *In the Spirit We're Equal,* Dr. Susan Hyatt has shown how this sort of thinking led to Christian women being treated as children and slaves. It also led to the beating of wives, which was often tolerated and even affirmed by the church.

Luther's marriage to Katy was, therefore, a wonderful departure from that way of thinking. Although he held to the traditional idea of the woman as the weaker vessel, he was too aware of human deficiency, including his own, to talk about male superiority.

The Lutheran scholar, Martin Brecht, says, "The marriage partners seemed to him to be equal." Luther, in fact, warned against either partner seeking dominance, saying,

> It is foolish for a man to want to demonstrate his masculine power and heroic strength by ruling over his wife. On the other hand, the ambition of wives to dominate the home is also intolerable.

Luther and Katy functioned according to their gifts. She obviously was a good manager and administrator, and he admitted that he wasn't. Her management of the household left him free to do that for which he was called and gifted. They functioned according to their gifts, not their gender.

If modern evangelicals would take a lesson from Luther and Katy, perhaps they could say, as Luther did, "There is no more lovely, friendly and charming relationship, communion or company than a good marriage."

Final Days

In later life, Luther was plagued with almost constant sickness, including chronic constipation, dysentery, kidney stones, ringing in his ears, fainting spells and bouts of depression. This led to an irritability and, no doubt, attributed to some of his ultra-harsh responses during this period, such as to the Jews.

In January of 1546, at the age of 63, Luther decided to make a trip to the place of his birth, Eisleben, and the place of his childhood, Mansfield. Because of poor health, his three sons, Hans, Martin and Paul, all teenagers, travelled with him, as did an assistant.

During the trip Luther became very ill and lost consciousness. His sons and the assistant rubbed him with warm towels until he revived. The symptoms he describes, tightness in the chest and heart palpitations, sounds like congestive heart failure. He continued the trip and was able even to stop and preach along the way.

He was staying in touch with Katy by mail and she obviously expressed deep concern and much anxiety for him. He responded to her, encouraging her not to worry, saying,

> I have a better Caretaker than you and all the angels.
> It is He who lies in a manger . . . but at the same time
> sits at the right hand of God, the almighty Father,
> Therefore, be at rest. Amen.[40]

He arrived in Eisleben, the place of his birth, weak in body but able to enjoy an evening meal with friends on February 17. He then retired to his room, but was restless and experiencing pain in his chest. His hosts gave him a herbal drink and he went off to sleep, but awakened an hour later still complaining of pain in his chest. He was also surprised to see many people in his room, for word had spread that Luther was dying.

Sensing that he was completing his time on earth, he began quoting Psalm 31:5, "Into your hands I commit my spirit. You have redeemed me God of truth." This Psalm was also quoted in part by Jesus on the cross. Luther then began to pray aloud thanking God that He had revealed His Son to him, "whom I have believed, whom I have loved, whom I have preached, confessed and praised."

He suddenly fell silent and seemed to be unconscious. Two friends, knowing that the manner of his death would be spread across Europe, shouted, "Revered father! Are you ready to die trusting in your Lord Jesus Christ and to confess the doctrine you have taught in His name?" Luther opened his mouth and in a clear voice spoke his final word, "Ja," meaning "Yes!" Fifteen minutes later, he was gone.[41]

Katie was heartbroken. Yet, in her pain, she knew the loss transcended her own personal sense of pain. She wrote,

> I am truly so deeply grieved that I cannot tell a single person of the great pain that is in my heart. I do not understand how I can cope with this. I cannot eat or drink, nor can I sleep. If I had a principality or an empire and lost it, it would not have been as painful as it is now that the dear Lord God has taken from

me this precious and beloved man, and not from me alone, but the whole world.

Luther's funeral in Wittenberg was attended by a mass throng of dignitaries and common folk from throughout the region. Melanchthon, his long-time friend and colleague at the University of Wittenberg, gave the eulogy in which he highlighted Luther's incredible impact on Christendom, saying,

> Many of us witnessed the struggles through which he passed in establishing the principles that by faith we are received and heard of God. Hence throughout eternity pious souls will magnify the benefits which He has bestowed on the Church through Luther.

Melanchthon also pointed out Luther's weaknesses but put them in the larger context of the age in which he ministered, and his spirit and intentions. He said,

> Some have complained that Luther displayed too much severity. I will not deny this. But I answer in the language of Erasmus, "Because of the magnitude of the disorders, God gave this age a violent physician." I do not deny that the more ardent characters sometimes make mistakes, for amid the weaknesses of human nature no one is without fault. But we may say of such a one, "rough indeed but worthy of all praise!" If he was severe, it was the severity of zeal for the truth, not the love of strife, or of harshness. God was his anchor and faith never failed him.

Chapter 6

Where Luther Fell Short

So if people want to see Luther as any kind of run
of the mill anti-Semite, they must be disappointed. He rightly
lays the blame for Jesus's Crucifixion, not on the Jews, but on
every one of us and on himself, as well he should.

Eric Metaxas

In II Corinthians 4:7 Paul says, *But we have this treasure in*
earthen vessels, that the excellence of the power may be of God and
not of us. Luther was certainly a man uniquely gifted and
prepared for such a time. His gifts, however, were
expressed through the "earthen vessel" of which Paul
speaks, exhibiting his human frailty, weakness and
shortcoming.

Luther was also a man of the times and a characteristic of
the times was the use of power and force, even in matters of
faith. This had been the case with the church since the time
of Constantine who merged the church with the state and
used the power of civil government to advance the cause of
the church.

Luther, in the beginning, rejected such use of force in
matters of faith However, his dependence on Frederick the
Wise for protection from the pope and emperor necessitated
the continuance of the medieval concept of a national
church in which the church is supported and upheld by the
state. In this political arrangement, the power of the state is

available to enforce the doctrines and practices of the official church.

Luther, no doubt, felt that Frederick the Wise, the powerful German prince, was a godsend to protect the Reformation in Germany. However, the establishment of Lutheranism as the official, state church of Germany became the basis for persecuting Catholics, Jews, Anabaptists and any group that was considered subversive to German Lutheranism.

Luther never advocated personal or vigilante violence, but he was convinced that the magistrate *does not bear the sword in vain*, as Paul put it in Romans 13:4. He believed that the civil authority had a responsibility, not only to maintain social order, but to also enforce the doctrines and practices of the church, an idea he retained from Roman Catholicism.

The establishment of Lutheranism as the official state church of Germany, also meant the continuance of the idea of the *corpus Christianum* in which church and society are essentially one, *i.e.*, a Christian society. And since infant baptism was the rite whereby a person became a bona fide member of the *corpus Christianum*, infant baptism was continued in the Lutheran churches.

Luther & the Anabaptists

The Anabaptists challenged this area of Luther's thinking, and came under the wrath of his pen. He recommended that they be silenced, arrested and expelled from Germany, because he considered their activities to be seditious and a threat to the peace o the nation.

The Anabaptists emerged out of the Reformation with those

who felt Luther was retaining too much of the old Roman Catholic system. They pointed, in particular, to Lutheranism being merged with the German state and the magistrate using force to maintain Lutheran doctrine and practice.

They insisted that the church should be free from the state and that there should be no use of force in matters of faith and worship. Because they took seriously Luther's emphasis on salvation by faith alone, they rejected infant baptism, reasoning that infants cannot exercise faith.

They replaced infant baptism with a believer's baptism administered at the time of the person making a conscious decision to put their faith in Christ. This then led to their rejection of the idea of a *corpus Christianum*, or Christian society. All societies, they insisted, include people who are not genuine Christians, in spite of their infant baptism.

The Anabaptists preached the gospel in Lutheran and Catholic areas, baptized those who received their message and gathered them as voluntary members into individual congregations. This was, however, considered seditious by both Catholics and Lutherans, and deserving of punishment

These Anabaptists called themselves "Brethren," carrying Luther's teaching on "the priesthood of all believers" to its logical conclusion, and dispensing with all hierarchy. They were given the label "Anabaptist," meaning "those who rebaptize," as a slur by Catholics and Lutherans who resented them rebaptizing their converts.

Luther defended the continuance of infant baptism, arguing

that God accepts the faith of the parents who bring their infant child for baptism. He used the gospel story of the men who brought their paralyzed friend to Jesus, and when Jesus saw "their" faith he spoke works of forgiveness and healing to the paralyzed man (Luke 5:20). In the same way, Luther said, God grants salvation to the infant on the basis of the faith of its parents.

Because of intense persecution by state-churches, both Catholic and Lutheran, the Anabaptists often met secretly in homes, forests or fields. There they read the Bible and prayed that the same Spirit and power that had been known by the primitive church would come upon them. It was thus not unusual for the Anabaptists to dance, fall under the power and speak in tongues.[42]

Most of the Anabaptists were peaceful evangelicals and some were even pacifists. There were, however, extremes that arose from their midst that blackened the name of the entire movement. In his dealings with the Anabaptists, Luther never distinguished between the different groups.

When Luther heard that Anabaptists were preaching in Germany, he reacted in anger, and in 1532, wrote a small book against them called, "Infiltrating and Clandestine Preachers." In this book Luther shows little understanding of the Anabaptists and refers to them as "regular thieves and murderers of souls, blasphemers and enemies of Christ and his churches." He also warned the populace to inform the civil authorities of the whereabouts of these infiltrators lest they be regarded as "accomplices in murder and revolt."[43]

Anabaptists were thus persecuted, imprisoned and expelled from Germany. The Anabaptist leaders had read Luther's writings and were aware that he was not offering them the same sort of freedom of conscience that he had demanded of the pope and the Roman Church. They, therefore, accused him of departing from his original teaching.

Luther, however, was merely being consistent with the idea of a national, state church, which he carried over from Roman Catholicism. In such an arrangement there can be only one ecclesiastical authority in a given region, and in Germany it was now Lutheranism.

The Anabaptist attempt to gather a believing church out of German society undermined this concept of a national church, and as far as Luther was concerned, amounted to nothing less than sedition and revolt against the established order. He, therefore, vehemently opposed them.

The Peasants' War

The medieval peasant was the scum of European society. They labored long and hard for minimal wages and were burdened down with heavy taxation, both legal and illegal. Their status was not much better than that of a slave, and they were oppressed by the aristocrats and nobles in both the state and the church.

Luther's attacks on the tyranny of the papacy and his rough and bold style resonated with the peasants and they identified with him. Luther also felt a certain affinity for the peasants and when they presented a list of demands to the rulers based on the justice, peace and charity of Christianity,

Luther sympathized with their cause.

When the rulers were slow in responding, Thomas Muntzer, the priest mentioned earlier from Zwickau, stirred them to take matters into their own hands. Muntzer preached a radical theology, similar to modern "liberation theology," in which he advocated the use of force to bring about the kingdom of God on earth. Through his agitation, and revolutionary ideology, violence broke out and spread across Germany with the peasants burning and looting.

Luther was against the use of force by individual Christians, but he believed the civil authority, according to Romans 13:1, had the divine right and responsibility to use the sword against evil. In his mind the peasant uprising was evil and needed to be put down by force.

He, therefore, took pen in hand and wrote a violent manifesto against "the rapacious and murderous peasants." He called upon the civil authorities to kill them like "mad dogs." He insisted that it was useless to reason with the peasants except by the fist and the sword.[44]

The war was brutal with over 100,00 lives lost. Over one-thousand castles and convents were burned, and hundreds of villages were burned to the ground. Whole districts were turned into a wilderness. Luther said, "Never has the aspect of Germany been more deplorable than now."

The Peasants' War and Luther's response to it resulted in Lutherans succumbing to a passive obedience to the civil authority, and trusting the civil authority to protect their cause. Luther's original ideals of individual freedom of conscience and religious liberty could only be carried so far in this setting.

It would be left to the more radical groups of the Reformation, the pacifist Anabaptists, Separatist Puritans and Quakers, who would formulate doctrines of the separation of church from state, freedom of conscience and individual liberty, and actually implement them in the New World that had just been discovered by Columbus.[45]

Luther & the Jews

The unfortunate consequences of a state church whose doctrines and practices are protected and enforced by the civil authority, spilled over into Luther's dealings with the Jews.

In the early days of the Reformation, Luther was very friendly toward the Jewish people and he maintained personal friendships with Jews throughout his life. He had hoped that Jews would respond *en masse* to the rediscovered gospel message of the Reformation.

In 1523 Luther wrote a book entitled, *That Jesus Christ Was Born a Jew*, in which he attempted to win Jews to Christ, and in that context, he also advocated humane treatment for them in the face of widespread anti-Semitism throughout Europe. He reminded Christians that Jesus Christ was born a Jew and that "we in turn ought to treat the Jews in a brotherly fashion." He also stated that he admired — indeed, loved — the Jewish people.

Luther reported on one occasion that three rabbis visited him because they had heard of his interest in the Hebrew language and hoped to reach an agreement with him.

However, they rejected Luther's argument that the messianic prophecies of the Old Testament point to Jesus Christ.

Nonetheless, because Jews were forbidden to travel in that part of Germany, Luther gave them a letter of introduction in which he asked, "for Christ's sake," that they be granted free passage. Because of his mention of Christ, they refrained from using the letter.

When his Jewish friend, Bernard, fell on hard times in 1531 and had to leave his family, Luther cared for one of his children and continued this support for many years. Luther said he did it because "he felt obligated to do good to Bernard as a member of the Jewish church." Bernard also served as a messenger for Luther on numerous occasions.

To another Jewish friend, Luther argued that the gospel had to be of God; for how else could it be explained that Gentiles, who hate Jews, worship a Jewish king, much less a crucified one.

Luther was eventually attacked by Jewish writers who vilified him for his attempts to win them to Christ. His writings such as, *That Jesus Christ Was Born a Jew*, were maligned and held up to ridicule.

Luther's response was, at first, mild. He replied, "For the sake of the crucified Jew, whom no one will take from me, I gladly wanted to do my best for you Jews, except that you abused my favor and hardened your hearts."

Luther's attitude toward the Jews obviously hardened as he entered more extensive dialogues/debates with Jewish rabbis on the Scriptures and the Messiah. Luther had hoped that, through these debates, the Jews would be won to faith in Christ.

Through these debates, however, Luther was exposed to writings that maligned Jesus and Christianity. He was horrified to read of Jesus being vilified as the illegitimate son of a whore and a cabalistic magician who was exposed for his trickery and put to death.

Having been taught from childhood to reverence and honor God and Jesus and Mary, he responded with both anger and fear. He wrote;

> I am still praying daily and I duck under the shelter of the Son of God. I hold Him and honor Him as my Lord, to whom I must run and flee when the devil, sin or other misfortune threatens me, for He is my shelter, as wide as heaven and earth, and my mother hen under whom I crawl from God's wrath. Therefore, I cannot have any fellowship or patience with obstinate blasphemers and those who defame this dear Savior.[46]

When he found the rabbis to be obstinate in their positions, he finally gave up any hope of the Jews coming to Christ *en masse*. And with them entertaining such blasphemous views of Christ, he gave up any hope of Christians and Jews being able to live together in harmony.

Although Luther should have responded in the spirit of the One he proclaimed (Who had prayed for His tormenters at the cross, "Father forgive them, they know not what they do") he, instead, reacted with anger and fury and wrote a treatise entitled *On the Jews and Their Lies*. The word *Lies* in the title referred to the Jewish diatribes against Jesus, Mary, and the Triune God. The third section of this book contains the diatribes that he fulminated against the Jewish people.

Different reasons have been offered for Luther's violent verbal attack on the Jews in which he called for their synagogues being burned and them being expelled from Germany. Some have pointed that this was just a few years before his death when he was dealing with various illnesses, including chronic constipation, dysentery, kidney stones, dizziness and bouts of depression. In this state, everything seemed to set him off.

Essentially, however, Luther related to the Jews the same way, and on the same basis, he did other groups with whom he disagreed. The rough, violent language he used against the Jews was the same sort of language he used against Anabaptists, Catholics, peasants, "Turks" and everyone he considered to be enemies of the gospel of Christ.

Luther is a prime example of how one's greatest strength may turn out to be their greatest weakness. His bold, bombastic rhetoric was exactly what was needed in confronting the pope, the emperor and the Roman Church. When, however, he was in a place of power and used the same rhetoric on weaker groups, that is when his greatest strength became his greatest weakness.

These verbal attacks were based on his belief that the magistrate had a Divine responsibility to enforce the doctrines and practices of the official church, which in Germany was Lutheranism. Dissenting belief systems were not tolerated. Therefore, Luther's attacks on Jews, Anabaptists, Turks and Catholics, were all doctrinal and theological in nature, not racial.

The eminent Lutheran scholar, Martin Brecht, makes this point as well, arguing that Luther's verbal attacks against the Jews were not based on race but on a disagreement in theology. He says that Luther, therefore, "was not involved with later racial anti-Semitism."[47]

Nonetheless, Luther's misguided invectives had the unfortunate result of him becoming identified with the church fathers of anti-Semitism and they provided fodder for modern anti-Semites who cloaked their hatred of the Jews in the authority of Luther.

On their website (www.lcms.org), The Lutheran Church, Missouri Synod, has graciously and wisely denounced Luther's anti-Jewish invectives while recognizing the vital and critical contributions he has made to all of Christendom.

They also point out Luther's conciliatory tone in his last sermon when he said of the Jews, "We want to treat them with Christian love and to pray for them, so that they might become converted and would receive the Lord." This indicates that, in later life, Luther's tone shifted back toward his earlier and more conciliatory attitude.

Another example of this occurred in 1545, about one year before his death, when he revised a hymn that had blamed the Jews for the death of Christ (a common claim by the medieval church). In his revision, Luther removed the invective against the Jews. His revised version reads,

T'was our great sins and misdeeds gross,
Nailed Jesus, God's true Son, to the cross.
Thus you, poor Judas, we dare not blame,
Nor the band of Jews; ours is the shame.

Commenting on this eye-opening revision by Luther, Eric Metaxas says,

> So if people want to see Luther as any kind of run of the mill anti-Semite, they must be disappointed. He rightly lays the blame for Jesus's Crucifixion not on the Jews, but on everyone one of us and on himself, as well he should.[48]

This author suspects that if Luther were living today in this more tolerant and civil era, and with the Jews back in their homeland, he might well be one of their biggest supporters.

Summary Statement

In summary, Luther's primary failure was in retaining the Constantinian concept of a national, state church. This, in turn, led to the use of force in matters of faith being carried over into the Reformation. Luther was never for individual or vigilante violence, but he did believe the civil magistrate had a Divine responsibility to maintain civil order and enforce the doctrines and practices of the Lutheran Church, even if it meant persecuting and expelling other groups.

It would be left to what George Williams called, the "Radical Reformers," to push for a separation, not of God and state, but of church and state. The Radical Reformers, beginning with the Anabaptists and continuing with the Separatist Puritans, English Baptists and Quakers, would insist on a state that protects the individual rights of all its citizens in matters of faith, without taking sides.

This was the ideal that Luther declared at the Diet of Worms. But it was the area where he fell short in carrying it through and applying it in real life. It would be left to his more radical contemporaries to formulate these radical doctrines of freedom of conscience and religious liberty and bring them to the New World where they would be the basis for the founding of a new nation.[49]

Chapter 7

The Legacy of Luther

But, with all his faults, he is the greatest man that Germany ever produced, and one of the very greatest in history. His influence extends far beyond the limits of his native land. He belongs to the church and the world. Melanchthon, who knew him best, called him the Elijah of Protestantism, and compared him to the Apostle Paul.

Philip Schaff, Historian

Even secular historians understand the significance of Luther. After the year 2000, the editors of *Life* magazine listed what they considered to be the one-hundred most important events of the past millennia. Luther's nailing of the 95 Theses to the Wittenberg Church door was listed at number two after the invention of the printing press in 1440, and before the discovery of America by Columbus in 1492, which was listed at number three.

Interestingly these top three events of the past thousand years all happened within a few short years of each other, and show the providential hand of God. The printing press was invented just in time to facilitate the demand for Bibles that would be instigated by Luther's emphasis of *sola Scriptura*. The discovery of America would open a new home for the children of the Reformation who would be severely persecuted by antagonistic civil and religious authorities in Europe.

Luther, therefore, despite his weaknesses, was a man uniquely prepared for a very unique moment in time. I have listed below five areas of his legacy that he has left the church and the world.

Number I
Courage to Stand for Truth

If Luther was anything, he was bold and courageous, so much so that his friends sometimes thought he was too bold. In giving a report to Spalatin about Luther's performance at the Diet of Worms, Frederick the Wise said, "How excellently did Father Martin speak before the Emperor and Estates. He was bold enough, if not too much so."[50]

It was, however, no time for timidity or reticence. The church was in shambles. God's people were enslaved to an oppressive religious system that was obsessed with power. The times called for a courageous voice that would not flinch in the face of the greatest powers on earth. Luther became that voice that God used to change the course of history.

Such bold voices are in great need in the church today. There is so much hedging, evading and ducking by Christian leaders today when it comes to making a clear sound for truth.

For example, this author was astounded to hear a well-known evangelical pastor and leader, dance in circles when asked by a popular TV icon if Jesus is the only way to God. Instead of giving a simple straightforward answer, he ducked, swerved and feinted, but never gave a clear answer to such a simple, straightforward question.

We have heard other leaders take the same approach of dodging and swerving when asked their views on abortion and same-sex marriage. One popular answer is, "We are having a conversation about that." My question is, "Why are you afraid to take a loving stand for truth?"

Contrast Luther, who in a letter to Pope Leo X dated September 6, 1520 and while still a Catholic priest, spoke with such clearness and boldness. He spoke with respect, even addressing Leo as "Holy Father," but he did not mince words. He wrote,

> I have truly despised your see, the Roman curia, which, however, neither you nor anyone else can deny is more corrupt than any Babylon or Sodom ever was, and which, as far as I can see, is characterized by a completely depraved, hopeless, and notorious godlessness.[51]

We can all be thankful that Luther did not duck, feint and dance around the issues of his day. He obviously made mistakes, but no one could ever complain of not knowing where he stood. He changed history by being clear, concise, courageous and bold.

May God raise up a generation to proclaim His truth with that same spirit of courage and boldness.

Number 2
Individual Freedom

Luther struck an incredible blow for individual freedom of conscience and religious liberty when at his trial for heresy he boldly resisted demands that he retract his teachings, declaring that "it is unsafe and dangerous to do anything against the conscience."[52] He went on to say, "My conscience is bound in the word of God, and I cannot and will not recant anything."[53]

Freedom of individual conscience was practically unheard of in the medieval world into which Luther was born. Individualism was suppressed. Conformity to the religious and social norms, determined by those in authority, was demanded and enforced.

Those who veered from the established religious norms were punished, imprisoned and even put to death. Individual freedom was sacrificed for what was considered the good of the whole by those in power. Most often, however, it was not for the good of the whole, but for the good of those in power, that individualism was suppressed.

By his bold stand at Worms, Luther unleashed a powerful ideal of individual freedom. Others took that ideal and brought it to America—the land of the free--where it was further developed on American soil.[54] Freedom of conscience and individual religious liberty then became hallmarks of freedom-loving people and nations throughout the Western world. We have Luther to thank for this.

Number 3
Back to the Bible – *Sola Scriptura*

When you hear a public figure quoting the Bible or hear how the Bible continues to be the perennial all-time best seller, you can thank Martin Luther. Luther directed the attention of the church back to the Bible as the ultimate guide and source of authority for morality, life and faith.

When George Washington, America's first president, insisted on taking the oath of office with his hand on a Bible, he was living out the legacy of Luther and *sola Scriptura*. When Washington declared, "It is impossible to rightly govern the world without God and the Bible,"[55] that was the influence and legacy of Luther.

In Luther's own life, the Bible was supreme. His boldness came from his conviction that Scripture is the highest authority to which one can appeal. When, therefore, he stood before the tribunal at Worms, his appeal was to Scripture. "My conscience is captive to the word of God," he declared.

Luther's high esteem for the Scriptures is expressed again and again in his writings. In his book, *To the German Nobility of the Christian Nation*, he wrote,

> I would advise no one to send his child where the Holy Scriptures are not supreme. Every institution that does not unceasingly pursue the study of God's word becomes corrupt.[56]

The popularity of Bible studies within Protestantism, and now also within Catholicism, can be traced to Luther and his emphasis on *sola Scriptura*. When modern evangelists, like Billy Graham, hold their Bible aloft and preface their statements with, "The Bible says," that is a direct legacy of Luther. Christians who are seen carrying their Bibles to church are acting in the legacy Luther.

Luther's priority of Scripture for the individual believer was something new and radical to the world of medieval Europe, which placed ultimate authority with the pope and church tradition. Luther's placement of Scripture as the final authority above church tradition and hierarchy was momentous for the history of the church and Western society.

Number 4
The Priesthood of All Believers

Luther's emphasis on the priesthood of all believers meant that the masses could go directly to God apart from the mediatorial priesthood of the medieval Roman Catholic Church. This was certainly good news for the masses who were held captive by a sacerdotal priesthood that claimed to be a necessary mediator between the people and God.

Now, the people could develop a personal relationship with God through Christ apart from the institutional church. This had far-ranging effects including the personal freedom to preach the gospel and begin new and unique congregations without the sanction of the religious institution.

Luther's adversaries accused him of creating chaos with this teaching. One individual, Johann Cochlaeus, complained,

> Even some women challenged theologians, and averred that all doctors were in darkness. Some of them were for mounting the pulpits and teaching in the churches. Had not Luther declared that by baptism we are all teachers, preachers, bishops, popes, etc.?

This statement shows how this teaching was giving women the boldness to move in areas that had, for centuries, been reserved for men only. Although there were, no doubt, extreme responses and applications of this teaching, the freedom brought about by its proclamation far outweighed any problems that were caused by its emphasis.

The most important aspect of this teaching on the priesthood of all believers was that it restored the Biblical truth that there is only one Mediator between God and humanity, and that is Jesus Christ (I Timothy 2:5). This released the masses from a religious fear and gave them faith to approach God on their own in personal faith.

The common phrase in evangelicalism, "a personal relationship with Jesus Christ," comes from Luther's emphasis on the priesthood of all believers. It is because individuals can go to God through Jesus Christ that they can have a personal relationship with Him apart from any earthly, religious priesthood. This was momentous for the explosive growth of Protestantism around the world.

Number 5
Opened the Way for Spiritual Awakening

With the masses now reading the Scriptures, particularly the New Testament, hearts were stirred to know and experience the Christianity of the Bible. This led to private and corporate times of prayer and more Bible study, as many sought a return to what was often called "primitive Christianity."

This search for the God of the Bible and the Christianity of the New Testament, opened the way for Spiritual awakenings that have been such a vital part of the Church since Luther. R. A. Torrey is correct to say, "The history of the Church of Jesus Christ on earth has been very largely a history of revivals," and this is especially true of the modern era.

The Methodist revival that shook the British Isles, the Great Awakenings that transformed colonial America and subsequent awakenings, would never have happened apart from Luther and his emphases on personal faith, Scripture and the priesthood of all believers.

The Methodist revival, in fact, began with John Wesley sitting in a Moravian meeting and listening to someone read Luther's *Preface to Romans*. Wesley recorded in his journal the powerful experience he had as he listened to Luther describe what happens when a person puts their faith in Christ alone for salvation. He wrote,

> I felt my heart strangely warmed. I felt I did trust in Christ, Christ alone for my salvation and an assurance was given me that He had taken away my sin, even mine, and saved me from the law of sin and death. [57]

Although historians normally emphasize Wesley's doctrine of holiness and sanctification, it was his preaching of *sola fide*, faith alone, that sparked the Methodist revival. As an ordained priest in the Church of England, Wesley began preaching that the way to God was through faith in Christ, not church sacraments and rituals. He caused quite a stir when he announced that he had only recently become a Christian, tracing his real conversion, not to his baptism or ordination, but to that time of hearing Luther's description of what happens when a person puts their faith in Christ alone.

This was also the case in New England where Jonathan Edwards read his Greek New Testament prayerfully and diligently. Out of his study, he was inspired to pray for a "revival of religion" in his region. God answered and the Great Awakening, that transformed colonial America and prepared her for statehood, broke forth in great majesty and power.

Yes, by his bold stand for truth, Luther removed human obstacles that had blocked the flow of the Holy Spirit for centuries. By breaking the back of religious tyranny and control, he helped open the way for the free flow of the Spirit in fulfillment of Acts 2:17, *And it shall come to pass in the last days, says God, I will pour out My spirit on all flesh.*

Conclusion

I will close this volume with an excerpt from Luther's great hymn, "A Might Fortress is Our God." These words show his deep faith in God and his belief that God's truth will ultimately triumph. He wrote,

> And though this world, with devils filled,
> Should **threaten** to undo us.
> We will not fear, for God hath willed,
> His truth to triumph through us.

May it be in Jesus' Name!

Endnotes

[1] Philip Schaff, vol. 7 of *History of the Christian Church* 8 vols. Grand Rapids: Eerdmans, 1910), 106.

[2] See Eddie Hyatt, *2000 Years of Charismatic Christianity* (Lake Mary, FL: 2002), 33-37.

[3] Schaff, vol. 7 of *History of the Christian Church*, 19.

[4] Schaff, vol. 6 of *History of the Christian Church*, 723.

[5] Schaff, vol. 6 of *History of the Christian Church*, 725.

[6] Schaff, vol. 7 of *History of the Christian Church*, 113.

[7] Schaff, vol. 7 of *History of the Christian Church*, 116.

[8] Schaff, vol. 7 of *History of the Christian Church*, 129

[9] Schaff, vol. 7 of *History of the Christian Church*, 130.

[10] Schaff, vol. 7 of *History of the Christian Church*, 130.

[11] George Cubitt, *The Life of Martin Luther* (New York: Carlton & Philips, 1853), 82.

[12] Martin Luther, "The Babylonian Captivity of the Church," *Three Treatises* (Philadelphia: Fortress Press, 1957), 194-95.

[13] Schaff, vol. 7 of *History of the Christian Church*, 180.

[14] Eric Metaxas, *Martin Luther* (New York: Viking, 2017), 178.

[15] Helmut T. Lehman, ed., vol. 34 of *Luther's Works*, 55 vols. (Philadelphia: Muhlenberg, 1958), 103.

[16] Schaff, vol. 7 of *History of the Christian Church*, 463.

[17] Martin Luther, "To the Christian Nobility of the German Nation," *Three Treatises* (Philadelphia: Fortress Press, 1957), 9-10.

[18] Martin Luther, "The Babylonian Captivity of the Church," *Three Treatises* (Philadelphia: Fortress Press, 1957), 194-95.

[19] Schaff, vol. 7 of *History of the Christian Church*, 175.

[20] Schaff, vol. 7 of *History of the Christian Church*, 383.

[21] Schaff, vol. 7 of *History of the Christian Church*, 299.

[22] Eddie Hyatt, *Revival Fire* (Tulsa: Hyatt Press, 2009), 86.

[23] Johann Mathesius, *Luthers Leben in Predigten* (Prague: herausgegeben von G. Loesche, 19060, 399; Quoted by John Horsch, "The Faith of the Swiss Brethren, II." *MQR* 5, no. 1 (1931): 16.

[24] Horsch, "The Faith of the Swiss Brethren,"

[25] Bengt Hoffman, *Luther and the Mystics* (Minneapolis: Augsburg, 1976), 190.

[26] Luther, "The Babylonian Captivity of the Church," *Three Treatises*, 202.

[27] John C. Oyer, *Lutheran Reformers Against the Anabaptists* (The Hague, Netherlands: Martinus Nijhoff, 1964), 231

[28] A. J. Gordon, *The Ministry of Healing* (Harrisburg, PA: Christian Publications, 1961), 92.

[29] Martin Brect, *Martin Luther: The Preservation of the Church, 1532-1536* (Minneapolis: Fortress Press), 235.

[30] *Change the World School of Prayer* (Studio City, NY: World Literature Crusade, 1976), C-35.

[31] Luther, "The Babylonian Captivity of the Church," *Three Treatises*, 255.

[32] Oyer, *Lutheran Reformers Against the Anabaptists, 234.*

[33] Stanley M. Burgess and Gary B. McGee, eds., *Dictionary of Pentecostal and Charismatic Movements*, (Grand Rapids: Zondervan, 1988), 565.

[34] Hyatt, *2000 Years of Charismatic Christianity*, 77.

[35] Hans Kung, *The Church* (Garden City, NY: Image Books, 1976), 257-58.

[36] Luther, "To the Christian Nobility of the German Nation," *Three Treatises*, 75-76.

[37] Schaff, vol. 7 of *History of the Christian Church*, 388.

[38] Martin Luther, *Table Talk* (Gainsville, FL: Logos-Bridge, 2004), 138-39.

[39] Schaff, vol. 7 of *History of the Christian Church*, 295.

[40] Metaxas, Martin *Luther*, 425.

[41] See Metaxas, Martin *Luther*, 425-28 for an excellent overview of Luther's death.

[42] Hyatt, 2000 *Years of Charismatic Christianity*, 79.

[43] Lehman, ed., vol. 6 of *Luther's Works*, 384-86.

[44] Schaff, vol. 7 of *History of* the *Christian Church*, 446-47.

[45] Eddie Hyatt, *Pilgrims and Patriots* (Grapevine, TX: Hyatt Press, 2016).

[46] Brect, *Martin Luther: The Preservation of the Church, 1532-1536,* 350.

[47] Brect, *Martin* Luther: *The Preservation of the Church, 1532-1536,* 351.

[48] Metaxas *Martin Luther*, 418.

[49] See my book, *Pilgrims and Patriots* (Grapevine, TX: Hyatt Press, 2016).

[50] Schaff, vol. 7 of History *of the Christian Church*, 307.

[51] Luther, "The *Freedom* of a Christian," *Three Treatises*, 268.

(Grand Rapids: Eerdmans, 1910, 304-05.

[53] Schaff, vol. 7 of *History of the Christian Church*, 304-05

[54] Hyatt, *Pilgrims and Patriots* (Grapevine, TX: Hyatt Press, 2016).

[55] Hyatt, *Pilgrims* and *Patriots, 137.*

[56] Luther, "To the Christian Nobility of the German Nation," *Three Treatises*, 100.

[57] Hyatt, 2000 *Years of Charismatic Christianity*, 101.

Selected Bibliography

Brecht, Martin. *Martin Luther: The Preservation of the Church, 1532-1536.* Minneapolis: Fortress Press,

Cubitt, George. *The Life of Martin Luther.* New York: Carlton & Philips, 1853.

Gordon, A.J. *The Ministry of Healing.* Harrisburg, PA: Christian Publications, 1961.

Lehman, Helmut T., Ed. *Luther's Works,* 55 vols. Philadelphia: Muhlenberg, 1958.

Hoffman, Bengt. *Luther and the Mystics.* Minneapolis: Augsburg, 1976.

Hyatt, Eddie. *2000 Years of Charismatic Christianity.* Lake Mary, FL, 2002.

___. *Pilgrims and Patriots.* Grapevine, TX: Hyatt Press, 2016.

Hyatt, Susan. *In the Spirit We're Equal.* Dallas: Hyatt Press, 1998.

Kung, Hans. *The Church.* Garden City, NY: Image Books, 1976.

Luther, Martin. *Three Treatises.* Philadelphia: Fortress Press, 1957.

___. *Table Talk.* Gainsville, FL: Logos-Bridge, 2004.

Metaxas, Eric. *Martin Luther.* New York: Viking, 2017.

Ritter, *Gerhard.* Trans. John Riches. *LUTHER His Life and Work.* New York: Harper & Row, 1959.

Schaff, Philip. *History of the Christian Church.* 8 vols. Grand Rapids: Eerdmans, 1910.

www.ingramcontent.com/pod-product-compliance
Lightning Source LLC
Chambersburg PA
CBHW032027040426

42448CB00006B/749